# 5

# american popular piano

## ETUDES

**Compositions by**
# Christopher Norton

**Additional Compositions and Arrangements**
# Dr. Scott McBride Smith

**Editor**
# Dr. Scott McBride Smith

**Associate Editor**
# Clarke MacIntosh

**Music**

Stratford, Ontario, Canada

# A Note about this Book

Pop music styles can be grouped into three broad categories:

■ **lyrical** — pieces with a beautiful singing quality and rich harmonies; usually played at a slow tempo;

■ **rhythmic** — more up-tempo pieces, with energetic, catchy rhythms; these often have a driving left hand part;

■ **ensemble** — works meant to be played with other musicians, or with backing tracks (or both!); this type of piece requires careful listening and shared energy.

**American Popular Piano** has been deliberately designed to develop skills in all three areas.

You can integrate the cool, motivating pieces in **American Popular Piano** into your piano studies in several ways.

■ pick a piece you like and learn it; when you're done, pick another!

■ choose a piece from each category to develop a complete range of skills in your playing;

■ polish a particular favorite for your local festival or competition. Works from **American Popular Piano** are featured on the lists of required pieces for many festivals and competitions;

■ use the pieces as optional contemporary selections in music examinations;

■ Or...just have fun!

Going hand-in-hand with the repertoire in **American Popular Piano** are the innovative **Etudes Albums** and **Skills Books**, designed to enhance each student's musical experience by building technical and aural skills.

■ **Technical Etudes** in both Classical and Pop Styles are based on musical ideas and technical challenges drawn from the repertoire. Practice these to improve your chops!

■ **Improvisation Etudes** offer an exciting new approach to improvisation that guides students effortlessly into spontaneous creativity. Not only does the user-friendly module structure integrate smoothly into traditional lessons, it opens up a whole new understanding of the repertoire being studied.

■ **Skills Books** help students develop key supporting skills in sight-reading, ear-training and technique; presented in complementary study modules that are both practical and effective.

Use all of the elements of **American Popular Piano** together to incorporate a comprehensive course of study into your everyday routine. The carefully thought-out pacing makes learning almost effortless. Making music and real progress has never been so much fun!

**Library and Archives Canada Cataloguing in Publication**

Norton, Christopher, 1953-

American popular piano [music] : etudes / compositions by Christopher Norton ;
additional compositions and arrangements, Scott McBride Smith ;
editor, Scott McBride Smith ; associate editor, S. Clarke MacIntosh.

To be complete in 11 volumes.
The series is organized in 11 levels, from preparatory to level 10, each including a repertoire album,
an etudes album, a skills book, and an instrumental backings compact disc.

ISBN 1-897379-11-0 (preparatory level).--ISBN 1-897379-12-9 (level 1).--
ISBN 1-897379-13-7 (level 2).--ISBN 1-897379-14-5 (level 3).--
ISBN 1-897379-15-3 (level 4).--ISBN 1-897379-16-1 (level 5)

1. Piano--Studies and exercises. I. Smith, Scott McBride II. MacIntosh, S. Clarke, 1959- III. Title.

MT225.N883A52 2006                    786.2                    C2006906214-5

# LEVEL 5 ETUDES
## Table of Contents

# Improv Etude - A Good Day

**MODULE 1**

**A** Play the backing track of *A Good Day*. The opening clicks represent ♩ (quarter notes).
After the clicks, clap ♩ with the track.

**B** Clap with the backing track:

**C** 1. Play *without* the backing track.
2. Play again *with* the backing track.

**D** 1. Play *without* the backing track.
2. Play again *with* the backing track.

**E** 1. Play *without* the backing track.
2. Play again *with* the backing track.

* Improv notes:

*swung 8ths*

* IMPROVISATION: *use this rhythm*

**5**

* use the Improv notes in any order.

* IMPROVISATION: *use this rhythm*

**9**

* use the Improv notes in any order.

**13**

Listen closely as you play your improvisation.
- Does each note sound good with the backing track?
- Are you keeping a steady beat and staying with the backing track?
Play several different improvisations and choose your favorite. Play it for your teacher.

**✔ Improv Tip:** *Compare mm. 1-2 with mm. 9-10 and notice the slight variation of the motif.*
*What variations can you do in your improvisation?*

# Improv Etude - A Good Day

**MODULE 2**

**A** Play the backing track of *A Good Day*. The opening clicks represent ♩ (quarter notes).
After the clicks, clap ♩ with the track.

**B** Clap with the backing track:

**C** 1. Play *without* the backing track.
2. Play again *with* the backing track.

**D** 1. Play *without* the backing track.
2. Play again *with* the backing track.

E  1. Play *without* the backing track.
   2. Play again *with* the backing track.

* Improv notes:

* use the Improv notes in any order.

* IMPROVISATION: *use this rhythm*

Listen closely as you play your improvisation.
 - Does each note sound good with the backing track?
 - Are you keeping a steady beat and staying with the backing track?
Play several different improvisations and choose your favorite. Play it for your teacher.

✔ **Improv Tip:** *Notice how you can use B♮ or B♭. Where do you think they sound best?*
*You can use them in the same measure if you like the sound!*

# Improv Etude - A Good Day

**MODULE 3**

**A** Play the backing track of *A Good Day*. The opening clicks represent ♩ (quarter notes).
After the clicks, clap ♩ with the track.

**B** Clap with the backing track:

**C** 1. Play *without* the backing track.
   2. Play again *with* the backing track.

**D** 1. Play *without* the backing track.
   2. Play again *with* the backing track.

**E** 1. Play *without* the backing track.
2. Play again *with* the backing track.

\* Improv notes:

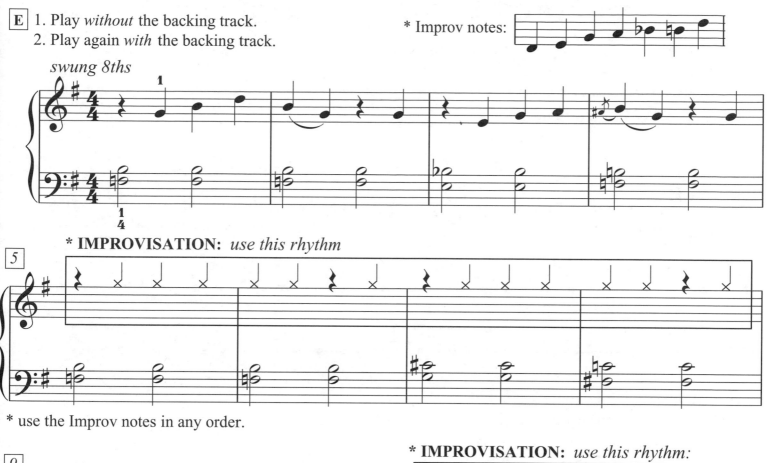

*swung 8ths*

\* **IMPROVISATION:** *use this rhythm*

\* use the Improv notes in any order.

\* **IMPROVISATION:** *use this rhythm:*

\* use the Improv notes in any order.

Listen closely as you play your improvisation.
- Does each note sound good with the backing track?
- Are you keeping a steady beat and staying with the backing track?
Play several different improvisations and choose your favorite. Play it for your teacher.

✔ **Improv Tip:** *Try accents on the fourth beat in your right hand to create momentum.*

# Improv Etude - A Good Day

**MODULE 4**

**A** Play the backing track of *A Good Day*. The opening clicks represent ♩ (quarter notes).
After the clicks, clap ♩ with the track.

**B** Clap with the backing track:

**C** 1. Play *without* the backing track.
2. Play again *with* the backing track.

**D** 1. Play *without* the backing track.
2. Play again *with* the backing track.

**E** 1. Play *without* the backing track.
2. Play again *with* the backing track.

\* Improv notes:

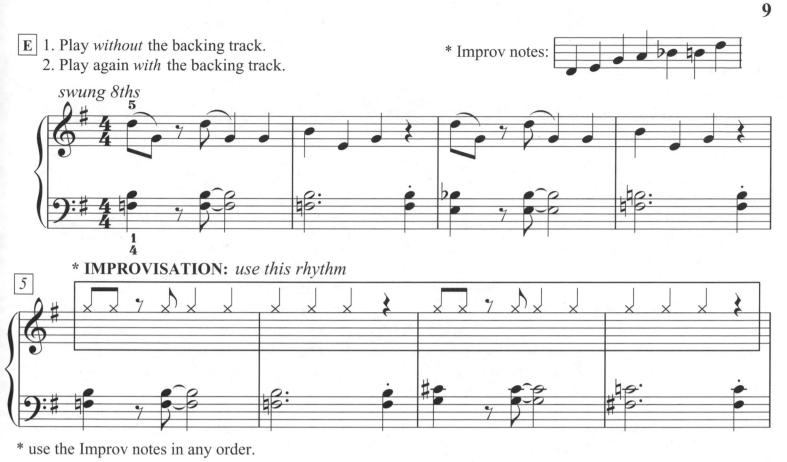

\* **IMPROVISATION:** *use this rhythm*

\* use the Improv notes in any order.

\* **IMPROVISATION:** *use this rhythm*

\* use the Improv notes in any order.

Listen closely as you play your improvisation.
- Does each note sound good with the backing track?
- Play several different improvisations and choose your favorite.
- Are you keeping a steady beat and staying with the backing track?

**✔** **Improv Tip:** *The left hand is playing quite an important part in this module - syncopated, then straight. Where is the syncopation in the improv section? How will you emphasize it in your improvisation?*

# Improv Etude - Workout

## MODULE 1

**A** Play the backing track of *Workout*. The opening clicks represent ♩ (quarter notes).

After the clicks, clap ♩ with the track.

**B** Clap with the backing track:

**C** 1. Play *without* the backing track.
2. Play again *with* the backing track.

**D** 1. Play *without* the backing track.
2. Play again *with* the backing track.

E 1. Play *without* the backing track.
2. Play again *with* the backing track.

* Improv notes:

* use the Improv notes in any order.

Listen closely as you play your improvisation.
- Does each note sound good with the backing track?
- Are you keeping a steady beat and staying with the backing track?
Play several different improvisations and choose your favorite. Play it for your teacher.

✔ **Improv Tip:** *The left hand is playing in triads, often moving in parallel motion.*
*Try first using chord tones in your improvisation, then add some dissonant notes.*

# Improv Etude - Workout

**MODULE 2**

**A** Play the backing track of *Workout*. The opening clicks represent ♩ (quarter notes).
After the clicks, clap ♩ with the track.

**B** Clap with the backing track:

*D.C. al coda*

**C** 1. Play *without* the backing track.
2. Play again *with* the backing track.

*D.C. al coda*

**D** 1. Play *without* the backing track.
2. Play again *with* the backing track.

*D.C. al coda*

**E** 1. Play *without* the backing track.
2. Play again *with* the backing track.

* Improv notes:

* use the Improv notes in any order.

*D.C. al coda*

Listen closely as you play your improvisation.
- Does each note sound good with the backing track?
- Are you keeping a steady beat and staying with the backing track?
Play several different improvisations and choose your favorite. Play it for your teacher.

✔ **Improv Tip:** *The left hand is mostly on the 'off' beats but the effect is good with the backing track! How does this affect your improvisation?*

# Improv Etude - Workout

**MODULE 3**

**A** Play the backing track of *Workout*. The opening clicks represent ♩ (quarter notes).

After the clicks, clap ♩ with the track.

**B** Clap with the backing track:

**C** 1. Play *without* the backing track.
2. Play again *with* the backing track.

**D** 1. Play *without* the backing track.
2. Play again *with* the backing track.

**E** 1. Play *without* the backing track.
2. Play again *with* the backing track.

\* Improv notes:

\* **IMPROVISATION:** *use this rhythm*

to Coda ⊕

\* use the Improv notes in any order.

*D.C. al coda*

⊕ **CODA**

Listen closely as you play your improvisation.
- Does each note sound good with the backing track?
- Are you keeping a steady beat and staying with the backing track?
Play several different improvisations and choose your favorite. Play it for your teacher.

✔ **Improv Tip:** *There are more sixteenth notes than usual, so you need to think faster!*

# Improv Etude - Workout

## MODULE 4

**A** Play the backing track of *Workout*. The opening clicks represent ♩ (quarter notes).
After the clicks, clap ♩ with the track.

**B** Clap with the backing track:

**C** 1. Play *without* the backing track.
2. Play again *with* the backing track.

**D** 1. Play *without* the backing track.
2. Play again *with* the backing track.

**E** 1. Play *without* the backing track.
2. Play again *with* the backing track.

\* Improv notes:

**\* IMPROVISATION:** *use this rhythm*

to Coda

\* use the Improv notes in any order.

*D.C. al coda*

CODA

Listen closely as you play your improvisation.
 - Does each note sound good with the backing track?
 - Are you keeping a steady beat and staying with the backing track?
Play several different improvisations and choose your favorite. Play it for your teacher.

✔ **Improv Tip:** *The left hand part should be rock steady, like a disco drummer.*
   *Equal accents on each beat are characteristic of this style.*

# Improv Etude - Breakfast Time

**MODULE 1**

**A** Play the backing track of *Breakfast Time* The opening clicks represent ♩ (quarter notes).
  After the clicks, clap ♩ with the track.

**B** Clap with the backing track:

**C** 1. Play *without* the backing track.
  2. Play again *with* the backing track.

**D** 1. Play *without* the backing track.
  2. Play again *with* the backing track.

E 1. Play *without* the backing track.
2. Play again *with* the backing track.

* Improv notes:

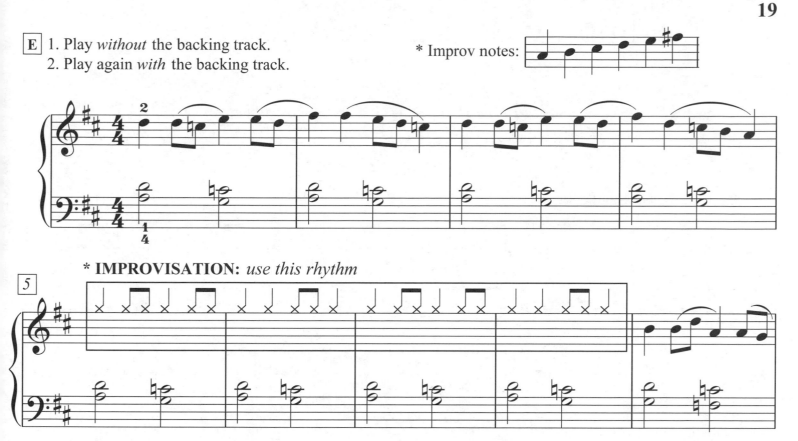

**\* IMPROVISATION:** *use this rhythm*

\* use the Improv notes in any order.

**\* IMPROVISATION:** *use this rhythm*

\* use the Improv notes in any order.

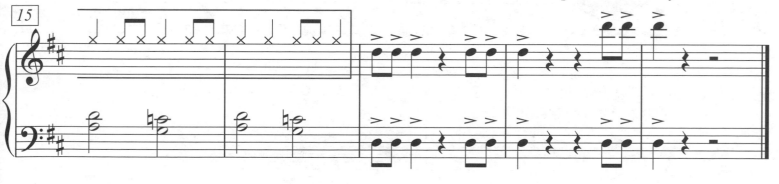

Listen closely as you play your improvisation.
 - Does each note sound good with the backing track?
 - Are you keeping a steady beat and staying with the backing track?
Play several different improvisations and choose your favorite. Play it for your teacher.

✔ **Improv Tip:** *The given melody has a repeated rhythm, but the notes are varied.*
     *Do you see any melodic patterns that you can use in your improvisation?*

# Improv Etude - Breakfast Time

**MODULE 2**

**A** Play the backing track of *Breakfast Time* The opening clicks represent ♩ (quarter notes).
  After the clicks, clap ♩ with the track.

**B** Clap with the backing track:

**C** 1. Play *without* the backing track.
  2. Play again *with* the backing track.

**D** 1. Play *without* the backing track.
  2. Play again *with* the backing track.

**E** 1. Play *without* the backing track.
2. Play again *with* the backing track.

* Improv notes:

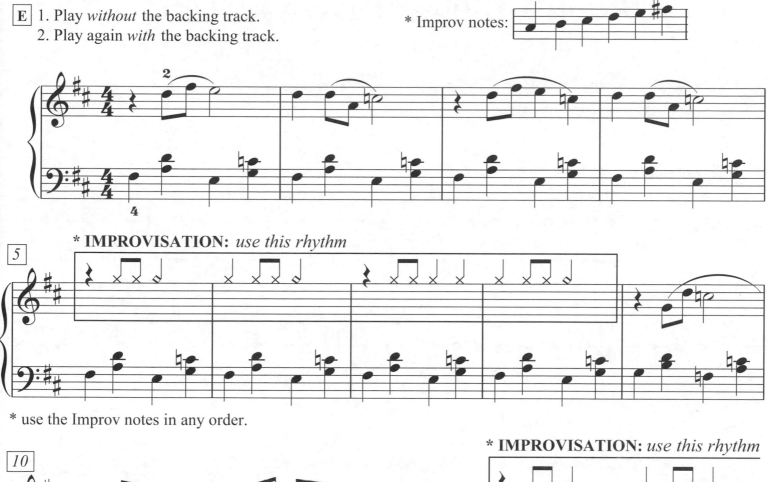

* use the Improv notes in any order.

* use the Improv notes in any order.

Listen closely as you play your improvisation.
  - Does each note sound good with the backing track?
  - Are you keeping a steady beat and staying with the backing track?
Play several different improvisations and choose your favorite.  Play it for your teacher.

**✔ Improv Tip:** *Notice how effective left hand chords can be when they are playing inversions.*
  *In your improvisation, try using those same chord tones, but in the opposite direction.*

# Improv Etude - Breakfast Time

**MODULE 3**

**A** Play the backing track of *Breakfast Time* The opening clicks represent ♩ (quarter notes).

After the clicks, clap ♩ with the track.

**B** Clap with the backing track:

**C** 1. Play *without* the backing track.
2. Play again *with* the backing track.

**D** 1. Play *without* the backing track.
2. Play again *with* the backing track.

**E** 1. Play *without* the backing track.
2. Play again *with* the backing track.

\* Improv notes:

\* use the Improv notes in any order.

\* use the Improv notes in any order.

Listen closely as you play your improvisation.
 - Does each note sound good with the backing track?
 - Are you keeping a steady beat and staying with the backing track?
Play several different improvisations and choose your favorite. Play it for your teacher.

**✔ Improv Tip:** *Are there any repeated measures in mm. 1-4?*
*Will you repeat anything in your improvisation?*

# Improv Etude - Breakfast Time

**MODULE 4**

24

A Play the backing track of *Breakfast Time* The opening clicks represent ♩ (quarter notes).

After the clicks, clap ♩ with the track.

B Clap with the backing track:

C 1. Play *without* the backing track.
2. Play again *with* the backing track.

D 1. Play *without* the backing track.
2. Play again *with* the backing track.

**E** 1. Play *without* the backing track.
2. Play again *with* the backing track.

\* Improv notes:

\* use the Improv notes in any order.

\* use the Improv notes in any order.

Listen closely as you play your improvisation.
- Does each note sound good with the backing track?
- Are you keeping a steady beat and staying with the backing track?
Play several different improvisations and choose your favorite. Play it for your teacher.

✔ **Improv Tip:** *Notice how cool it sounds to double the accents from the backing track in the melody.*

# Improv Etude - Grizzly

**MODULE 1**

**A** Play the backing track of *Grizzly*. The opening clicks represent ♩ (quarter notes).

 After the clicks, clap ♩ with the track.

**B** Clap with the backing track:

**C** 1. Play *without* the backing track.
 2. Play again *with* the backing track.

**D** 1. Play *without* the backing track.
 2. Play again *with* the backing track.

E  1. Play *without* the backing track.
2. Play again *with* the backing track.

* Improv notes:

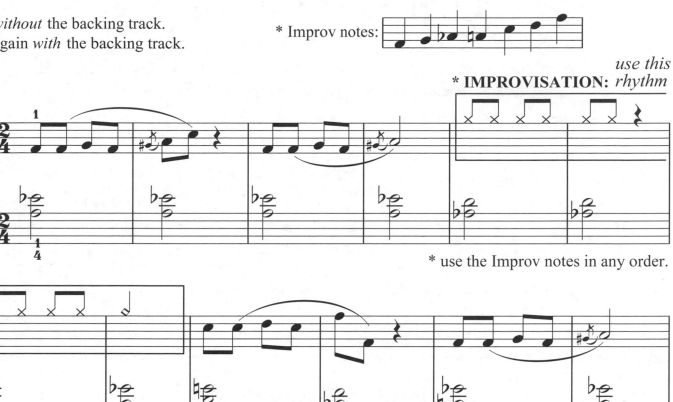

*use this*
**\* IMPROVISATION:** *rhythm*

\* use the Improv notes in any order.

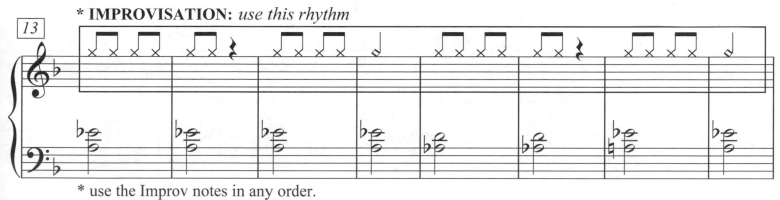

\* use the Improv notes in any order.

Listen closely as you play your improvisation.
- Does each note sound good with the backing track?
- Are you keeping a steady beat and staying with the backing track?
Play several different improvisations and choose your favorite.  Play it for your teacher.

✔ **Improv Tip:** *Grace notes can be very effective, especially in blues-style pieces like* Grizzly.

# Improv Etude - Grizzly

## MODULE 2

**A** Play the backing track of *Grizzly*. The opening clicks represent ♩ (quarter notes).

After the clicks, clap ♩ with the track.

**B** Clap with the backing track:

**C** 1. Play *without* the backing track.
2. Play again *with* the backing track.

**D** 1. Play *without* the backing track.
2. Play again *with* the backing track.

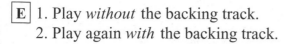 **E** 1. Play *without* the backing track.
2. Play again *with* the backing track.

* Improv notes:

*use this*
* **IMPROVISATION:** *rhythm*

* use the Improv notes in any order.

* **IMPROVISATION:** *use this rhythm*

* use the Improv notes in any order.

Listen closely as you play your improvisation.
- Does each note sound good with the backing track?
- Are you keeping a steady beat and staying with the backing track?
Play several different improvisations and choose your favorite. Play it for your teacher.

✔ **Improv Tip:** *Try substituting all the A♭'s for A♮'s and all the A♮'s for A♭'s.*
*The alternating gives a "bluesy" feel - so experiment to find the balance you like.*

# Improv Etude - Grizzly

**MODULE 3**

**A** Play the backing track of *Grizzly*. The opening clicks represent ♩ (quarter notes).
After the clicks, clap ♩ with the track.

**B** Clap with the backing track:

**C** 1. Play *without* the backing track.
2. Play again *with* the backing track.

**D** 1. Play *without* the backing track.
2. Play again *with* the backing track.

E 1. Play *without* the backing track.
   2. Play again *with* the backing track.

* Improv notes:

*use this*
* **IMPROVISATION:** *rhythm*

* use the Improv notes in any order.

* **IMPROVISATION:** *use this rhythm*

* use the Improv notes in any order.

Listen closely as you play your improvisation.
 - Does each note sound good with the backing track?
 - Are you keeping a steady beat and staying with the backing track?
Play several different improvisations and choose your favorite. Play it for your teacher.

✔ **Improv Tip:** *It's worth practicing the left hand with the track so that it feels absolutely natural to be "off beat". Let the interplay between the hands inspire your improvisation.*

# Improv Etude - Grizzly

**MODULE 4**

**A** Play the backing track of *Grizzly*. The opening clicks represent ♩ (quarter notes).
After the clicks, clap ♩ with the track.

**B** Clap with the backing track:

**C** 1. Play *without* the backing track.
2. Play again *with* the backing track.

**D** 1. Play *without* the backing track.
2. Play again *with* the backing track.

**E** 1. Play *without* the backing track.
2. Play again *with* the backing track.

* Improv notes:

*use this*
* **IMPROVISATION:** *rhythm*

* use the Improv notes in any order.

**7**

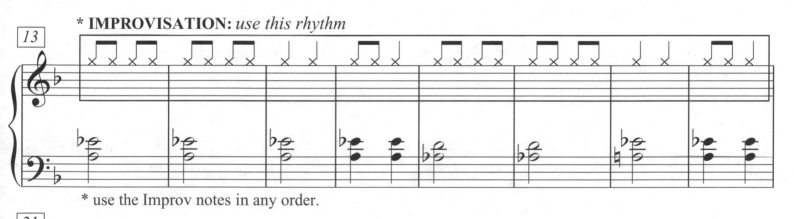

* **IMPROVISATION:** *use this rhythm*

**13**

* use the Improv notes in any order.

**21**

Listen closely as you play your improvisation.
- Does each note sound good with the backing track?
- Are you keeping a steady beat and staying with the backing track?
Play several different improvisations and choose your favorite. Play it for your teacher.

✔ **Improv Tip:** *Notice how the tied left hand notes add "punch" to your performance.*
*You can use tied notes in the right hand, too.*

# Improv Etude - It Takes Two

**MODULE 1**

**A** Play the backing track of *It Takes Two*. The opening clicks represent ♩ (quarter notes).
After the clicks, clap ♩ with the track.

**B** Clap with the backing track:

**C** 1. Play *without* the backing track.
2. Play again *with* the backing track.

**D** 1. Play *without* the backing track.
2. Play again *with* the backing track.

**E** 1. Play *without* the backing track.
2. Play again *with* the backing track.

* Improv notes:

### * IMPROVISATION:
*use this rhythm*

* use the Improv notes in any order.

Listen closely as you play your improvisation.
 - Does each note sound good with the backing track?
 - Are you keeping a steady beat and staying with the backing track?
Play several different improvisations and choose your favorite.  Play it for your teacher.

✔ **Improv Tip:** *This is the first use of this scale for improvisation.  What scale is it?*

# Improv Etude - It Takes Two

**MODULE 2**

**A** Play the backing track of *It Takes Two*. The opening clicks represent ♩ (quarter notes).

After the clicks, clap ♩ with the track.

**B** Clap with the backing track:

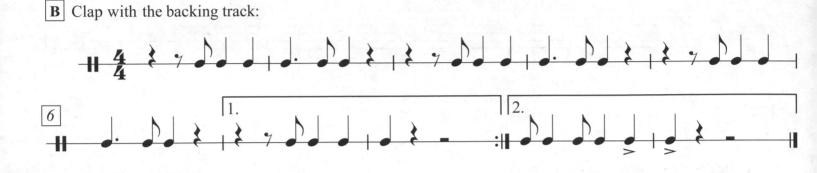

**C** 1. Play *without* the backing track.
   2. Play again *with* the backing track.

**D** 1. Play *without* the backing track.
   2. Play again *with* the backing track.

E 1. Play *without* the backing track.
2. Play again *with* the backing track.

* Improv notes:

**\* IMPROVISATION:**
*use this rhythm*

* use the Improv notes in any order.

Listen closely as you play your improvisation.
- Does each note sound good with the backing track?
- Are you keeping a steady beat and staying with the backing track?
Play several different improvisations and choose your favorite. Play it for your teacher.

✔ **Improv Tip:** *You might consider keeping the melodic ideas simple so that the focus is on
the rhythmic interplay between the hands when you do your improvisation.*

# Improv Etude - It Takes Two

**MODULE 3**

**A** Play the backing track of *It Takes Two*. The opening clicks represent ♩ (quarter notes).
After the clicks, clap ♩ with the track.

**B** Clap with the backing track:

**C** 1. Play *without* the backing track.
2. Play again *with* the backing track.

**D** 1. Play *without* the backing track.
2. Play again *with* the backing track.

E  1. Play *without* the backing track.
   2. Play again *with* the backing track.

* Improv notes:

**\* IMPROVISATION:**
*use this rhythm*

\* use the Improv notes in any order.

Listen closely as you play your improvisation.
  - Does each note sound good with the backing track?
  - Are you keeping a steady beat and staying with the backing track?
Play several different improvisations and choose your favorite.  Play it for your teacher.

✔ **Improv Tip:** *Here the left hand has gaps at the same places as the right hand.*
             *How does that affect the feeling of your improvisation?*

# Improv Etude - It Takes Two

**MODULE 4**

**A** Play the backing track of *It Takes Two*. The opening clicks represent ♩ (quarter notes).
After the clicks, clap ♩ with the track.

**B** Clap with the backing track:

**C** 1. Play *without* the backing track.
2. Play again *with* the backing track.

**D** 1. Play *without* the backing track.
2. Play again *with* the backing track.

**E** 1. Play *without* the backing track.
2. Play again *with* the backing track.

* Improv notes:

**\* IMPROVISATION:**
*use this rhythm*

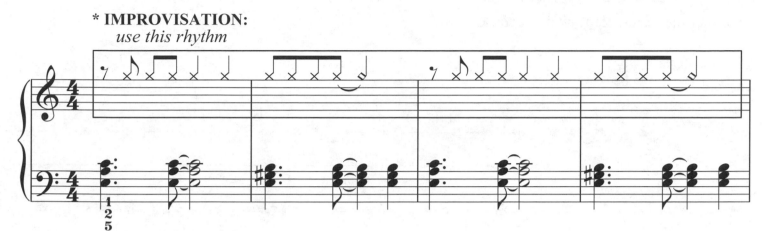

* use the Improv notes in any order.

Listen closely as you play your improvisation.
- Does each note sound good with the backing track?
- Are you keeping a steady beat and staying with the backing track?
Play several different improvisations and choose your favorite.  Play it for your teacher.

✔ **Improv Tip:** *Make the most of crisp articulation when you improvise.  Accents add energy, too.*

# Improv Etude - Left Behind

**MODULE 1**

**A** Play the backing track of *Left Behind*. The opening clicks represent ♩ (quarter notes).
After the clicks, clap ♩ with the track.

**B** Clap with the backing track:

**C** 1. Play *without* the backing track.
2. Play again *with* the backing track.

**D** 1. Play *without* the backing track.
2. Play again *with* the backing track.

**E** 1. Play *without* the backing track.
2. Play again *with* the backing track.

\* Improv notes:

**\* IMPROVISATION:**
*use this rhythm*

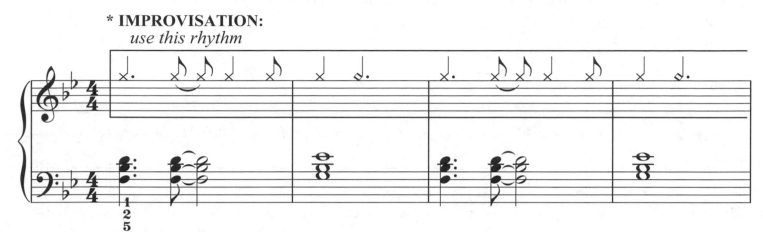

\* use the Improv notes in any order.

Listen closely as you play your improvisation.
 - Does each note sound good with the backing track?
 - Are you keeping a steady beat and staying with the backing track?
Play several different improvisations and choose your favorite. Play it for your teacher.

✔ **Improv Tip:** *Make your improvisations smooth and natural-sounding.*
   *Don't be afraid to repeat a motif if it is a good one.*

# Improv Etude - Left Behind

**MODULE 2**

**A** Play the backing track of *Left Behind.* The opening clicks represent ♩ (quarter notes).
After the clicks, clap ♩ with the track.

**B** Clap with the backing track:

**C** 1. Play *without* the backing track.
2. Play again *with* the backing track.

**D** 1. Play *without* the backing track.
2. Play again *with* the backing track.

**E** 1. Play *without* the backing track.
2. Play again *with* the backing track.

\* Improv notes:

**\* IMPROVISATION:**
*use this rhythm*

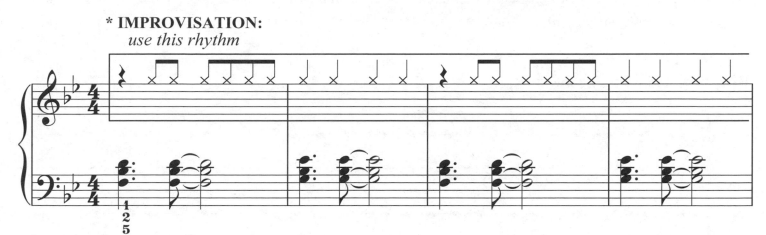

\* use the Improv notes in any order.

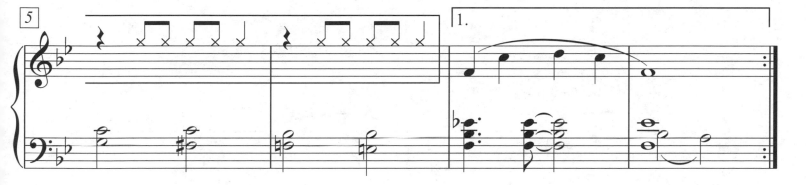

Listen closely as you play your improvisation.
- Does each note sound good with the backing track?
- Are you keeping a steady beat and staying with the backing track?
Play several different improvisations and choose your favorite. Play it for your teacher.

✔ **Improv Tip:** *This piece uses a sophisticated chord progression.*
*How does this affect your choice of melody notes?*

# Improv Etude - Left Behind

**MODULE 3**

**A** Play the backing track of *Left Behind.* The opening clicks represent ♩ (quarter notes).
After the clicks, clap ♩ with the track.

**B** Clap with the backing track:

**C** 1. Play *without* the backing track.
2. Play again *with* the backing track.

**D** 1. Play *without* the backing track.
2. Play again *with* the backing track.

E 1. Play *without* the backing track.
2. Play again *with* the backing track.

* Improv notes:

**\* IMPROVISATION:**
*use this rhythm*

\* use the Improv notes in any order.

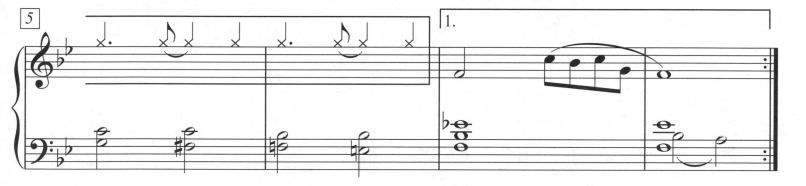

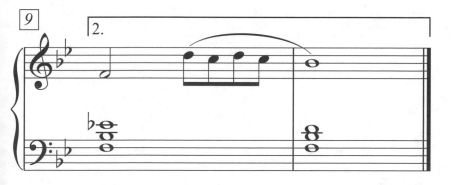

Listen closely as you play your improvisation.
  - Docs cach notc sound good with the backing track?
  - Are you keeping a steady beat and staying with the backing track?
Play several different improvisations and choose your favorite.  Play it for your teacher.

✔ **Improv Tip:** *All of the left hand chords are inversions.  How does this affect the mood*
*of the piece?  Your improvised melody should complement the feeling.*

# Improv Etude - Left Behind

**MODULE 4**

**A** Play the backing track of *Left Behind.* The opening clicks represent ♩ (quarter notes).
After the clicks, clap ♩ with the track.

**B** Clap with the backing track:

**C** 1. Play *without* the backing track.
2. Play again *with* the backing track.

**D** 1. Play *without* the backing track.
2. Play again *with* the backing track.

**E** 1. Play *without* the backing track.
2. Play again *with* the backing track.

\* Improv notes:

**\* IMPROVISATION:**
*use this rhythm*

\* use the Improv notes in any order.

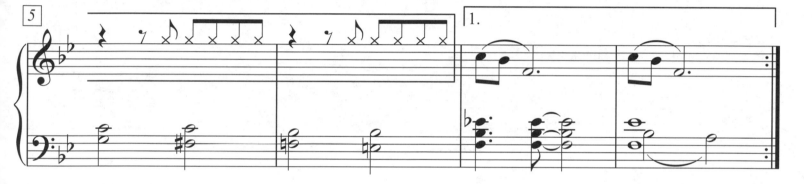

Listen closely as you play your improvisation.
   - Does each note sound good with the backing track?
   - Are you keeping a steady beat and staying with the backing track?
Play several different improvisations and choose your favorite. Play it for your teacher.

✔ **Improv Tip:** *Repetition and sequence are both great improvisation tools.*

# Improv Etude - Floating Away

**MODULE 1**

**A** Play the backing track of *Floating Away*. The opening clicks represent ♩ (quarter notes).

After the clicks, clap ♩ with the track.

**B** Clap with the backing track:

**C** 1. Play *without* the backing track.
2. Play again *with* the backing track.

**D** 1. Play *without* the backing track.
2. Play again *with* the backing track.

E 1. Play *without* the backing track.
2. Play again *with* the backing track.

\* Improv notes:

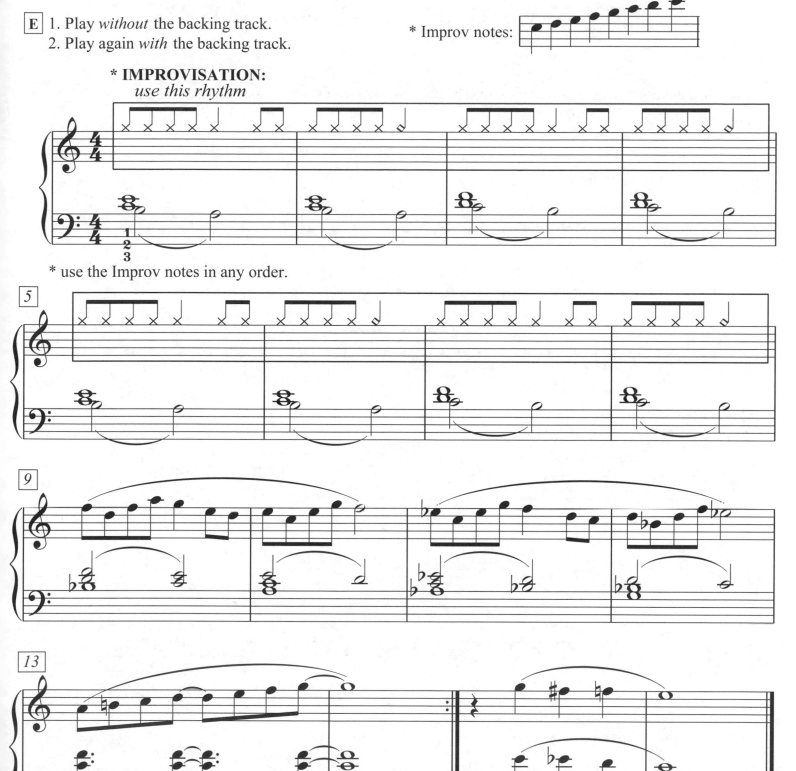

\* **IMPROVISATION:**
*use this rhythm*

\* use the Improv notes in any order.

Listen closely as you play your improvisation.
 - Does each note sound good with the backing track?
 - Are you keeping a steady beat and staying with the backing track?
Play several different improvisations and choose your favorite. Play it for your teacher.

✔ **Improv Tip:** *This is a longer piece than previous ones. Try building longer phrases in your melody.*

# Improv Etude - Floating Away

**MODULE 2**

**A** Play the backing track of *Floating Away*. The opening clicks represent ♩ (quarter notes).

After the clicks, clap ♩ with the track.

**B** Clap with the backing track:

**C** 1. Play *without* the backing track.
2. Play again *with* the backing track.

**D** 1. Play *without* the backing track.
2. Play again *with* the backing track.

E  1. Play *without* the backing track.
   2. Play again *with* the backing track.

* Improv notes: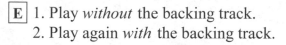

Listen closely as you play your improvisation.
  - Does each note sound good with the backing track?
  - Are you keeping a steady beat and staying with the backing track?
Play several different improvisations and choose your favorite. Play it for your teacher.

✔ **Improv Tip:** *The left hand has many sequences - try some in your right hand.*

# Improv Etude - Floating Away

**MODULE 3**

**A** Play the backing track of *Floating Away*. The opening clicks represent ♩ (quarter notes).
After the clicks, clap ♩ with the track.

**B** Clap with the backing track:

**C** 1. Play *without* the backing track.
2. Play again *with* the backing track.

**D** 1. Play *without* the backing track.
2. Play again *with* the backing track.

E 1. Play *without* the backing track.
2. Play again *with* the backing track.

* Improv notes:

**\* IMPROVISATION:** *use this rhythm*

* use the Improv notes in any order.

Listen closely as you play your improvisation.
- Does each note sound good with the backing track?
- Are you keeping a steady beat and staying with the backing track?
Play several different improvisations and choose your favorite. Play it for your teacher.

✔ **Improv Tip:** *The left hand in mm. 5-8 is the same as in mm. 1-4. Should your melody be the same, too?*

# Improv Etude - Floating Away

**MODULE 4**

**A** Play the backing track of *Floating Away*. The opening clicks represent ♩ (quarter notes).

After the clicks, clap ♩ with the track.

**B** Clap with the backing track:

**C** 1. Play *without* the backing track.
2. Play again *with* the backing track.

**D** 1. Play *without* the backing track.
2. Play again *with* the backing track.

E 1. Play *without* the backing track.
2. Play again *with* the backing track.

* Improv notes:

* use the Improv notes in any order.

Listen closely as you play your improvisation.
- Does each note sound good with the backing track?
- Are you keeping a steady beat and staying with the backing track?
Play several different improvisations and choose your favorite. Play it for your teacher.

✔ **Improv Tip:** *Notice that only white notes are used for the improvisation. What mood does this create?*

# Improv Etude - The Showman

**MODULE 1**

**A** Play the backing track of *The Showman.* The opening clicks represent ♩ (quarter notes).

After the clicks, clap ♩ with the track.

**B** Clap with the backing track:

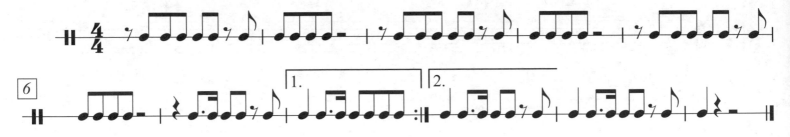

**C** 1. Play *without* the backing track.
2. Play again *with* the backing track.

**D** 1. Play *without* the backing track.
2. Play again *with* the backing track.

E  1. Play *without* the backing track.
2. Play again *with* the backing track.

* Improv notes:

**\* IMPROVISATION:**
*use this rhythm*

\* use the Improv notes in any order.

Listen closely as you play your improvisation.
- Does each note sound good with the backing track?
- Are you keeping a steady beat and staying with the backing track?
Play several different improvisations and choose your favorite.  Play it for your teacher.

✔ **Improv Tip:** *You are doubling the off-beat organ chords on the backing with your left hand.*
*How will you play your melody to create balance?*

# Improv Etude - The Showman

## MODULE 2

**A** Play the backing track of *The Showman.* The opening clicks represent ♩ (quarter notes).
After the clicks, clap ♩ with the track.

**B** Clap with the backing track:

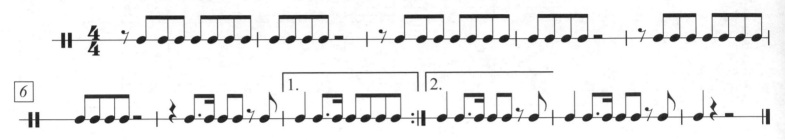

**C** 1. Play *without* the backing track.
2. Play again *with* the backing track.

**D** 1. Play *without* the backing track.
2. Play again *with* the backing track.

E  1. Play *without* the backing track.
2. Play again *with* the backing track.

\* Improv notes:

\* IMPROVISATION:
*use this rhythm*

\* use the Improv notes in any order.

Listen closely as you play your improvisation.
- Does each note sound good with the backing track?
- Are you keeping a steady beat and staying with the backing track?
Play several different improvisations and choose your favorite.  Play it for your teacher.

✔ **Improv Tip:** *Notice how effective it is to double the big brass riff at the end of each section.*
*Do you think you should play your improvisation lightly to create contrast?*

# Improv Etude - The Showman

**MODULE 3**

**A** Play the backing track of *The Showman*. The opening clicks represent ♩ (quarter notes).

After the clicks, clap ♩ with the track.

**B** Clap with the backing track:

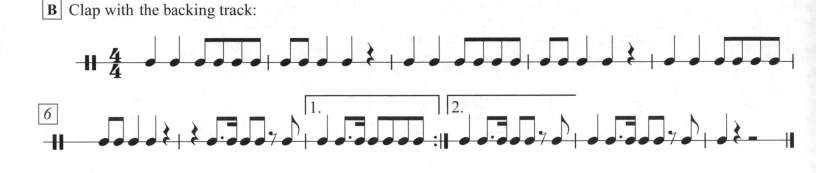

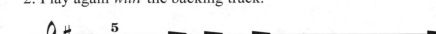

**C** 1. Play *without* the backing track.
2. Play again *with* the backing track.

**D** 1. Play *without* the backing track.
2. Play again *with* the backing track.

1. Play *without* the backing track.
2. Play again *with* the backing track.

\* Improv notes:

**\* IMPROVISATION:**
*use this rhythm*

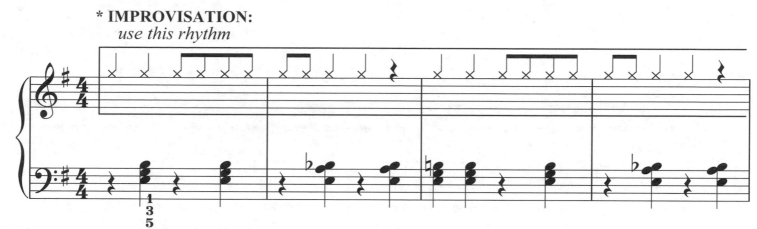

\* use the Improv notes in any order.

Listen closely as you play your improvisation.
- Does each note sound good with the backing track?
- Are you keeping a steady beat and staying with the backing track?
Play several different improvisations and choose your favorite. Play it for your teacher.

✔ **Improv Tip:** *Think in sixteenth notes right from the beginning.*
*That way, at m. 7 you will be exactly rhythmic.*

# Improv Etude - The Showman

**MODULE 4**

**A** Play the backing track of *The Showman.* The opening clicks represent ♩ (quarter notes).

After the clicks, clap ♩ with the track.

**B** Clap with the backing track:

**C** 1. Play *without* the backing track.
2. Play again *with* the backing track.

**D** 1. Play *without* the backing track.
2. Play again *with* the backing track.

E
1. Play *without* the backing track.
2. Play again *with* the backing track.

\* Improv notes:

**\* IMPROVISATION:**
*use this rhythm*

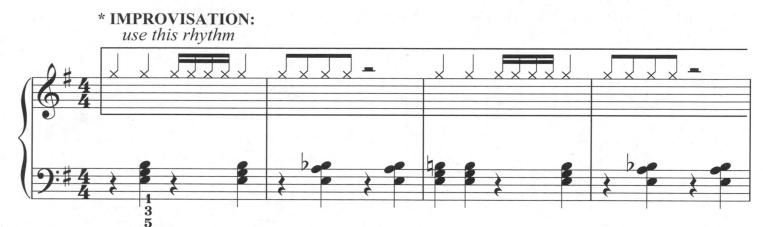

\* use the Improv notes in any order.

Listen closely as you play your improvisation.
 - Does each note sound good with the backing track?
 - Are you keeping a steady beat and staying with the backing track?
Play several different improvisations and choose your favorite.  Play it for your teacher.

✔ **Improv Tip:** *This is the first sixteenth note improvisation.*
                    *Keep your melodic ideas simple at first.*

# Performance Etude - A Good Day

**A** Practice the *A Good Day* Performance Etude based on the notes and rhythms you have already used in the modules. Once this feels comfortable, experiment with your own rhythms. Do this several times.

Improv notes:

**B** Work on your improvisation without the backing track until you can play with a steady tempo. Then practice with the backing track. Choose your favorite version and play it for your teacher.

Listen closely as you play your improvisation.
- Does each note sound good with the backing track?
- Are you keeping a steady beat and staying with the backing track?

**✔ Improv Tip:** *What beats do the groups of four 8th notes start on in mm. 1-4? You can start your improvisation motifs on the same beats.*

# Performance Etude - Workout

**A** Practice the *Workout* Performance Etude based on
the notes and rhythms you have already used in the modules.
Once this feels comfortable, experiment with your own rhythms.
Do this several times.

Improv notes:

**B** Work on your improvisation without the backing track until you can play with a steady tempo.
Then practice with the backing track. Choose your favorite version and play it for your teacher.

Listen closely as you play your improvisation.
- Does each note sound good with the backing track?
- Are you keeping a steady beat and staying with the backing track?

✔ **Improv Tip:** *Your performance should positively crackle with energy!*
*Use rests, accents, and syncopations to make it "pop".*

# Performance Etude - Breakfast Time

**A** Practice the *Breakfast Time* Performance Etude based on
the notes and rhythms you have already used in the modules.
Once this feels comfortable, experiment with your own rhythms.
Do this several times.

Improv notes:

**B** Work on your improvisation without the backing track until you can play with a steady tempo.
Then practice with the backing track. Choose your favorite version and play it for your teacher.

Listen closely as you play your improvisation.
- Does each note sound good with the backing track?
- Are you keeping a steady beat and staying with the backing track?

✔ **Improv Tip:** *This piece is in Mixolydian mode - D major with a flattened C - which can suit many moods.*
*Experiment with ideas that provide contrast.*

# Performance Etude - Grizzly

**A** Practice the *Grizzly* Performance Etude based on
the notes and rhythms you have already used in the modules.
Once this feels comfortable, experiment with your own rhythms.
Do this several times.

Improv notes:

**B** Work on your improvisation without the backing track until you can play with a steady tempo.
Then practice with the backing track. Choose your favorite version and play it for your teacher.

Listen closely as you play your improvisation.
- Does each note sound good with the backing track?
- Are you keeping a steady beat and staying with the backing track?

✔ **Improv Tip:** *Enjoy the silences as much as the notes! Rests are a key part of improvisation.*

# Performance Etude - It Takes Two

**A** Practice the *It Takes Two* Performance Etude based on the notes and rhythms you have already used in the modules. Once this feels comfortable, experiment with your own rhythms. Do this several times.

Improv notes:

**B** Work on your improvisation without the backing track until you can play with a steady tempo. Then practice with the backing track. Choose your favorite version and play it for your teacher.

**Tango style**

Listen closely as you play your improvisation.
- Does each note sound good with the backing track?
- Are you keeping a steady beat and staying with the backing track?

**✔ Improv Tip:** *You can be quite dramatic with your improv on this one. Pretend you are a Spanish soldier!*

# Performance Etude - Left Behind

**A**   Practice the *Left Behind* Performance Etude based on
the notes and rhythms you have already used in the modules.
Once this feels comfortable, experiment with your own rhythms.
Do this several times.

Improv notes:

**B**   Work on your improvisation without the backing track until you can play with a steady tempo.
Then practice with the backing track. Choose your favorite version and play it for your teacher.

Listen closely as you play your improvisation.
- Does each note sound good with the backing track?
- Are you keeping a steady beat and staying with the backing track?

✔ **Improv Tip:** *When the track is playing, don't get* Left Behind*! Feel the beat before you start.*

# Performance Etude - Floating Away

**A** Practice the *Floating Away* Performance Etude based on the notes and rhythms you have already used in the modules. Once this feels comfortable, experiment with your own rhythms. Do this several times.

Improv notes:

**B** Work on your improvisation without the backing track until you can play with a steady tempo. Then practice with the backing track. Choose your favorite version and play it for your teacher.

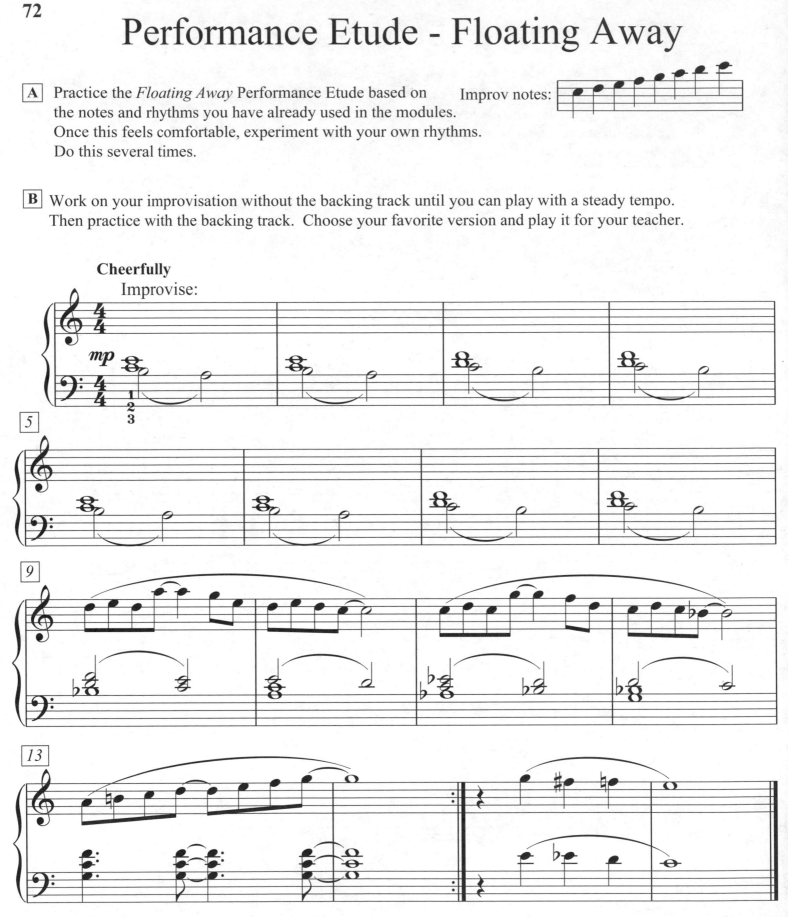

Listen closely as you play your improvisation.
- Does each note sound good with the backing track?
- Are you keeping a steady beat and staying with the backing track?

✔ **Improv Tip:** *This piece has a very "easy" feel - the rhythm is relaxed and you should be too! Keep it smooth and flowing throughout.*

# Performance Etude - The Showman

**A** Practice the *The Showman* Performance Etude based on
the notes and rhythms you have already used in the modules.
Once this feels comfortable, experiment with your own rhythms.
Do this several times.

Improv notes:

**B** Work on your improvisation without the backing track until you can play with a steady tempo.
Then practice with the backing track. Choose your favorite version and play it for your teacher.

**Strutting**

Listen closely as you play your improvisation.
- Does each note sound good with the backing track?
- Are you keeping a steady beat and staying with the backing track?

**✔ Improv Tip:** *Make your improvisation rhythmic and dramatic!*

# Moderato

Duvernoy

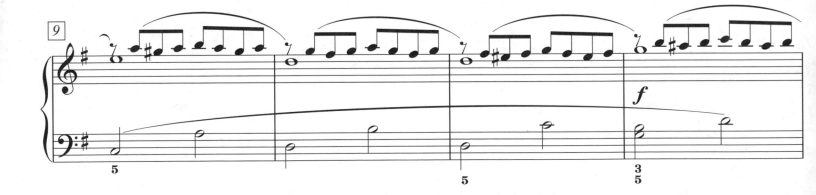

# Allegretto

F. Le Couppey

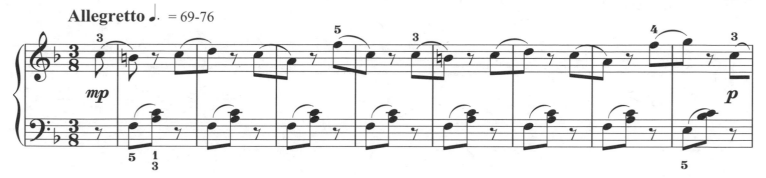

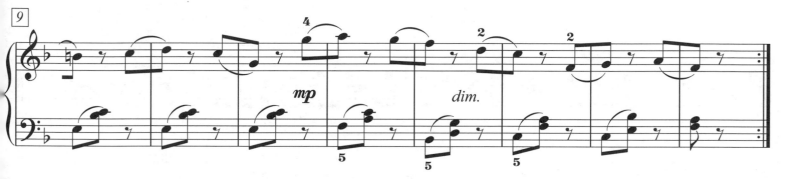

# Allegretto

C. Mayer

# Allegretto

C. Czerny

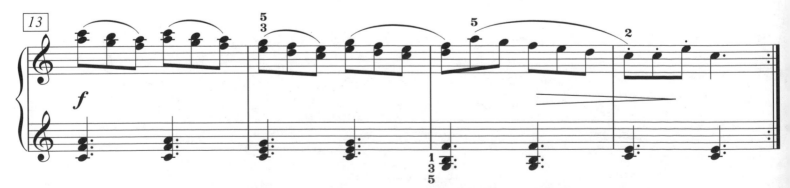

# Allegretto

C. Gurlitt

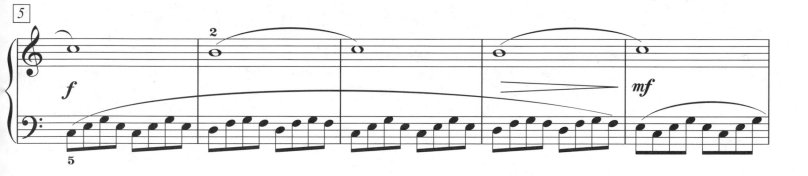

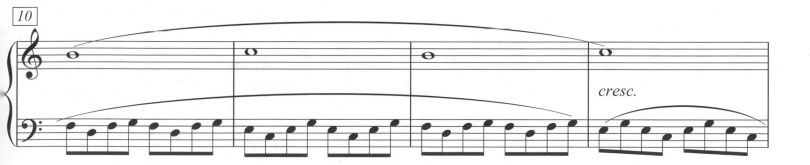

# Moderato

C. Stamaty

# Allegro

C. Czerny

# Allegro

L. Schytte

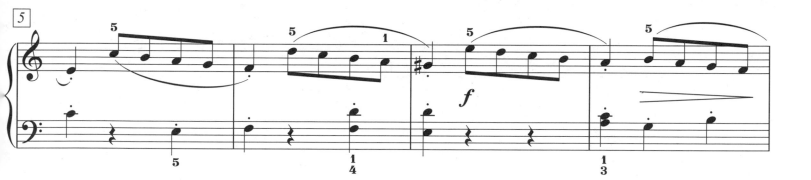

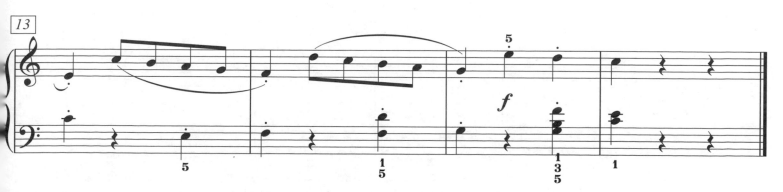

# Fishpond

Christopher Norton

# The Darkening Clouds

Christopher Norton

# Early Morning Run

Christopher Norton

# The Bell Ringer

Christopher Norton

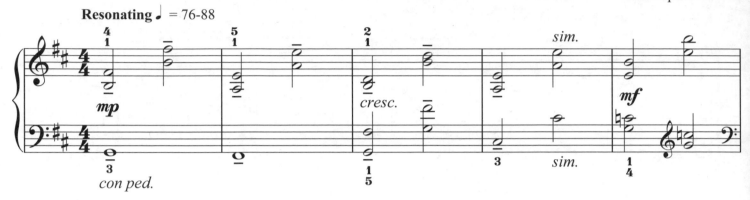

# My Best Day

Christopher Norton

# A Little Bossa

Christopher Norton

# All For One

Christopher Norton

# Around The Park

Christopher Norton

# LEVEL 5 ETUDES
## Glossary

**Backbeat** ....... Emphasis on beats 2 and 4, in a 4-beat bar. Usually accented by the drums, the backbeat is the most common rhythm in rock music.

**Beguine** ........ A type of Rumba in which the accent is on the second eighth note of the first beat. The style often has strong rhythms supporting flowing, sensuous melodies. Examples include: *Tropical Groove, Begin the Beguine*

**Blues** .......... Musical genre created by African-American musicians, with "blues" notes played against a major-key chord progression often using chords I, IV and V. Examples include: *Heartbreak Hotel*

**Blues notes** .... A pattern based on a major scale with flat 3rd, 5th, and 7th notes.

**Blues shuffle** .. A blues chord progression in 12/8, propelled along by the bass or piano left hand. Examples include: *Locomotive Blues, Hound Dog*

**Bossa nova** .... A Brazilian dance style, with a 2+3+3 eighth note pattern in the right hand over a dotted quarter note, eighth note pattern in the left hand, often with rich, sensuous chords. Examples include: *The Girl from Ipanema*

**Call and response** ... A style of singing in which the melody sung by one singer is echoed or "answered" by another. Examples include: *My Generation*

**Calypso** ........ A popular song form from the Caribbean island of Trinidad, generally upbeat. Popularized by Harry Belafonte, calypso has an emphasis on acoustic guitars and a variety of percussion instruments, particularly claves, shaker, and bongos. Examples include: *Banana Boat Song*

**Cha cha** ........ An exciting syncopated Latin dance, with a characteristic "cha cha cha" rhythm at the end. Examples include: *Never on a Sunday*

**Country Swing** . A combination of country, cowboy, polka, and folk music, blended with a jazzy "swing", featuring pedal steel guitar. Examples include: *Lovesick Blues* (Hank Williams)

**Disco** .......... An up-tempo style of dance music that originated in the early 1970s, derived from funk and soul music. Examples include: *Workout, Staying Alive*

**8-beat rock** .... A staple rock 'n' roll rhythmic pattern with 8 eighth notes in every bar featuring strong accents on beats 2 and 4. The accents are usually emphasized by the drums.

**Funk (funky)** ... A musical style associated with James Brown. The bass features 16th note pickups to the beat, with flourishes of 16th note syncopations in the bass and horns against a rock backbeat. Examples include: *Get on Up*

**Gospel** ......... An African-American religious style featuring a solo singer with heavily ornamented, simple melodies and a dramatic, wide vocal range. The soloist is often accompanied by a choir providing a rich harmonic backdrop. Examples include: *Nobody Knows the Trouble I've Seen*

**Jazz** ............ Jazz encompasses New Orleans Dixieland from the early 1900's, New York stride piano of the 1930's, big-band music from the 1940's, Chicago blues of the 1950's, and atonal free-form music of the 1960's. Jazz has its origins in uniquely American musical traditions, is generally based on chord structures of popular songs from the 1920's to the present, and always features some improvisation.

**Jazz ballad** ..... A song-like jazz style, often for solo piano, with rich chords and an emphasis on beauty of tone. Jazz ballads can be played either as solos or with bass and drums providing support. Examples include: *Jazz Hymn, My Foolish Heart*

**Jazz waltz** ...... A generally relaxed swing style in 3/4 time. Examples include: *Picnic, Moon River*

**Motown** ........ A style of soul music which originated in Detroit, whose features include the use of tambourine along with drums and a "call and response" singing style derived from gospel music. Examples include: *Motor City, ABC*

**Pop ballad** ..... A form of slow love song prevalent in nearly all genres of popular music. There are various types of pop ballad, from sixteenth-note ballads, to eight-beat ballads, to swing ballads. There is generally an emphasis on romance in the lyrics. Examples include: *A Matter of Regret, Kiss from a Rose*

**Reggae** ......... A music style from Jamaica, with elements of calypso, rhythm and blues, and characterized by a strong offbeat. Examples include: *Jamaican Market, No Woman No Cry*

**Rhythm and blues** ....... A style of music that combines blues and jazz, characterized by a strong off-beat and variations on syncopated instrumental phrases.

**Shuffle** ......... Based on the tap dancing style where the dancer, wearing soft-soled shoes, "shuffles" their feet in a swung 8ths rhythm. Examples include: *Train Stop, Lido Shuffle*

**16-beat ballad** A song-based style with gentle momentum created by continuous 16th notes in the rhythm, usually provided by the hi-hat cymbal. Examples include: *Killing Me Softly*

**Soul** ............ An African-American style combining elements of gospel music and rhythm and blues.

**Stomp** .......... A lively, rhythmic jazz style marked by a heavy beat. The style derives its name from the stamping of the pianist's heel along with the beat. Examples include: *Grizzly, Black Bottom Stomp* (Jelly Roll Morton)

**Swing** .......... A fun, dance-like style, usually using swung 8ths.

**Swung 8ths** .... 8th notes that are written normally, but played in this gentle dotted rhythm:

**Tango** .......... A rhythmically strict style, with no off-beat and a snare roll on beat 4. Examples include: *It Takes Two, Hernando's Hideaway*

**Thriller feel** .... Named after the title song on Michael Jackson's Thriller album, this style has a distinctive bass line and rhythmic feel. The funky bass plays against an 8-beat rock rhythm in a minor key. Examples include: *Bad*

**Walking bass** .. A bass style which has a note on every quarter note beat of the bar, usually "walking" from one beat to the next in scale tones (either whole or half steps) or along arpeggiated chords. Examples include: *Taking Things in Stride*

**Waltz** .......... A dance in 3/4 time, usually played with a strong accent on the first beat, with weaker beats on beats 2 and 3 in the accompaniment. Examples include: *Edelweiss*